WOMEN Wonderfully MADE

GIRL'S BOOK

written by
ALICIA HERNON

the
messy family
project®

Dear Mom,

We are so happy you have purchased this book because it is our desire that this tool begin a new and deeper relationship between you and your daughter. She needs you as a guide for the transitions she is going through now, in the coming months, and even in the years ahead.

This book is designed to accompany the Mother's Book that is purchased separately. If you would like even more resources for this course, you can scan the code here to check them out!

At the link, you will find a printable My Personal Proverbs chart referenced in the book, coloring pages for your daughter, and some sample clips of our course videos.

Our course videos are designed to accompany this book. Some moms are comfortable presenting information about adolescence in their own words, and if that describes you, great! We are happy that you have this guide. But if you'd rather not have the pressure, I can present the information so you can sit with your daughter, follow along with the book, and answer her questions, then check out our videos!

Either way, welcome to Women Wonderfully Made, and we hope you are enriched by what you discover in this daughter's workbook and companion mother's teaching guide. By the end, we hope that both of you are inspired to give thanks to our Heavenly Father Who made every woman perfectly and wonderfully.

In Him,

Alicia and the Messy Family Project team

I praise You, because I am wonderfully made; wonderful are Your works!

Why are we doing this course?

To be ready for the changes coming

One of the biggest changes you will go through in your life is the transition from girlhood to womanhood. For some girls, this time can be full of questions, worry, or even fear, but the way to conquer these feelings is through gaining wisdom by understanding. Wisdom and understanding can help us avoid unnecessary suffering and carry the suffering we can't escape with dignity and even joy. There is nothing that we can't handle with God's help!

Knowing about your body, learning what is normal and what is not, and growing in your relationship with your mom and other women will help this transition be a time of growth not just physically, but spiritually and emotionally as well.

We want you to connect with your own mom in understanding this plan, and with other girls and women so you can learn and seek wisdom together. Understanding our bodies and ourselves, enables us to more deeply appreciate our calling as women.

What am I most looking forward to in this course?

Today

NOW DRAW A PICTURE OF YOU AND YOUR
MOM 10 YEARS FROM NOW.

10 years
FROM NOW

To take responsibility for our bodies

When you were a baby, your mom and dad did everything for you! They fed you, dressed you, and changed your diaper. But now, you do all those things for yourself (except for the diaper part, I hope!). As you grew, you took more and more responsibility for yourself. In this course, we are going to talk about how you can support your body in the big changes that are coming. This is important because you will need to take care of your body your whole life! This is part of growing up.

Why is your feminine body so important? Because you, along with every woman, were created to bear life within you! **This is our superpower!**

> "The moral and spiritual strength of a woman is joined to her awareness that God entrusts the human being to her in a special way."
>
> **ON THE DIGNITY AND VOCATION OF WOMEN**

Because our bodies have the amazing ability to nurture life, we need to be very aware of how we use our body, how we feed our body, and how we care for our body. A woman's body is complex and intricately designed, and it needs to be cared for very intentionally. At times, problems that women experience with their bodies have to do with the lack of care that they give it. In this course we will talk about how you can start now to take responsibility for the beautiful body God has given you.

How do I take responsibility for myself now? What do I do to care for my body?

....

....

....

....

....

....

....

....

....

What do I want to learn more about?

....

....

....

....

....

....

....

....

To praise God that you are wonderfully made!

God made you a woman. It was His choice. Up until now, it might have seemed a little random—why are you a girl and not a boy? The simple answer is that God chose to create you as a girl. He gave you a female body, and as you grow, He will begin to show you the wonderful and exciting plan He has for you as a woman.

Being a woman doesn't mean wearing pink or liking sparkling things. It doesn't mean wearing skirts or high heels. Being a woman means we are honored by God to have the capacity to bring forth life. Men have not been given this gift! Each of us was born inside another woman: our mothers! Being a woman means being part of the human race that brings the rest of us into existence. This is not something we should resent or hate or fear. It's something that we should praise God for.

God designed our bodies with particular care. **We are His crown of creation**—the last thing God created, according to the Bible, was woman, and it's clear we are meant to be His masterpiece. Following the example of Mary, our Blessed Mother, we can learn to fully embrace how we have been made by our perfect Heavenly Father and join with her in praising God for being "fearfully and wonderfully made!"

Write a statement of praise to God for how He made you!

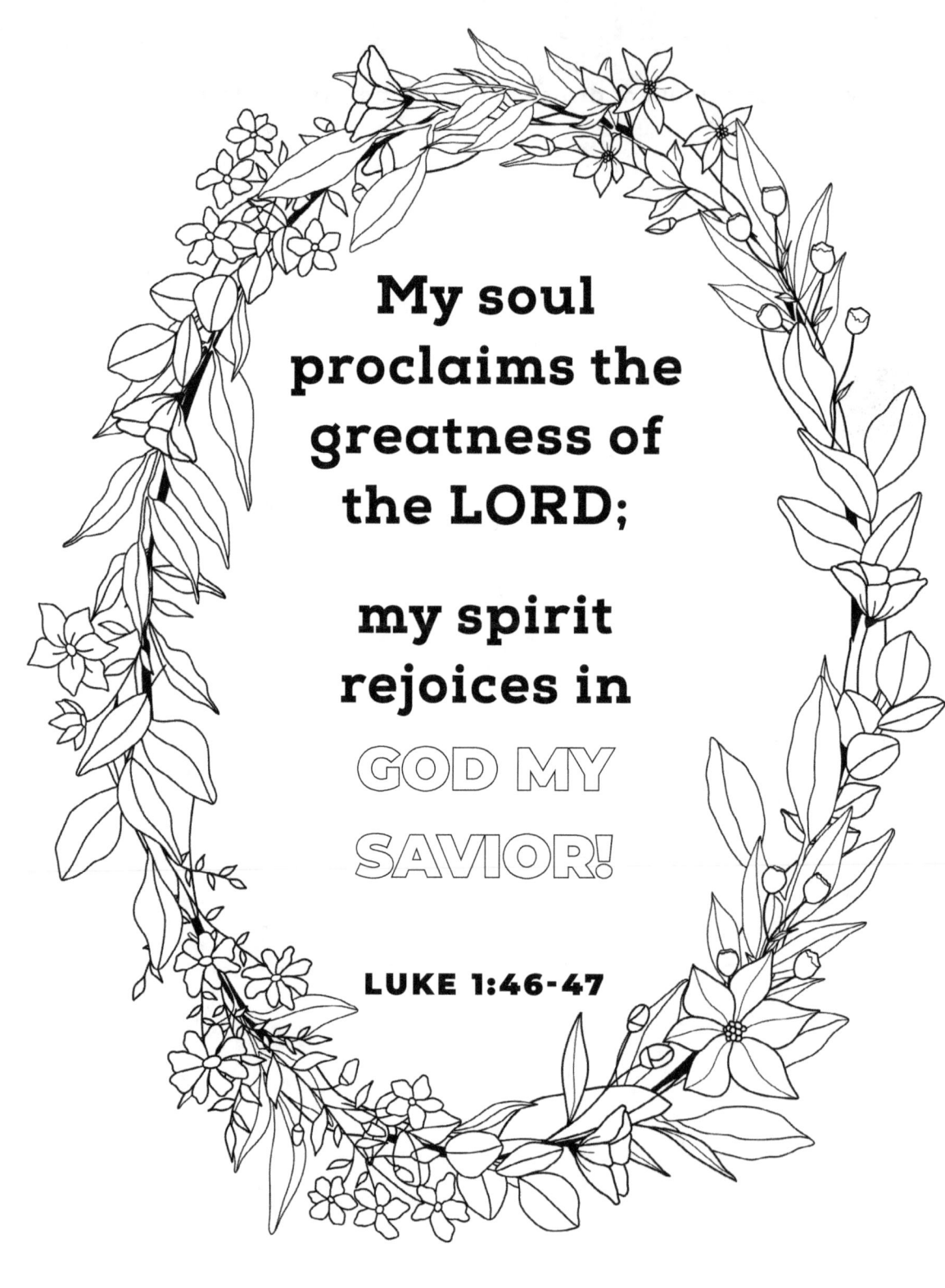

My soul
proclaims the
greatness of
the LORD;

my spirit
rejoices in

GOD MY
SAVIOR!

LUKE 1:46-47

Wonderfully Made - Our Body's Design

We all have a body—there are bodies everywhere we look! So in some ways, bodies are very ordinary. But we are called by God to see ourselves and others differently. We are all actually quite extraordinary! **Women especially have a design that reveals the presence of a Creator,** a loving and infinitely wise Father, Who has a plan for each of us. And His design is amazing!

> "'The revelation of the body' helps us in some way to discover the extraordinary nature of what is ordinary."
>
> **ST. JOHN PAUL II**

Basic Body Design

You probably know what your body looks like from the outside: now we will be discussing what it looks like from the inside. Here are some of the organs in your body, including the reproductive system as well as other systems so you can see where things are placed.

THE FEMALE BODY - SIDE VIEW

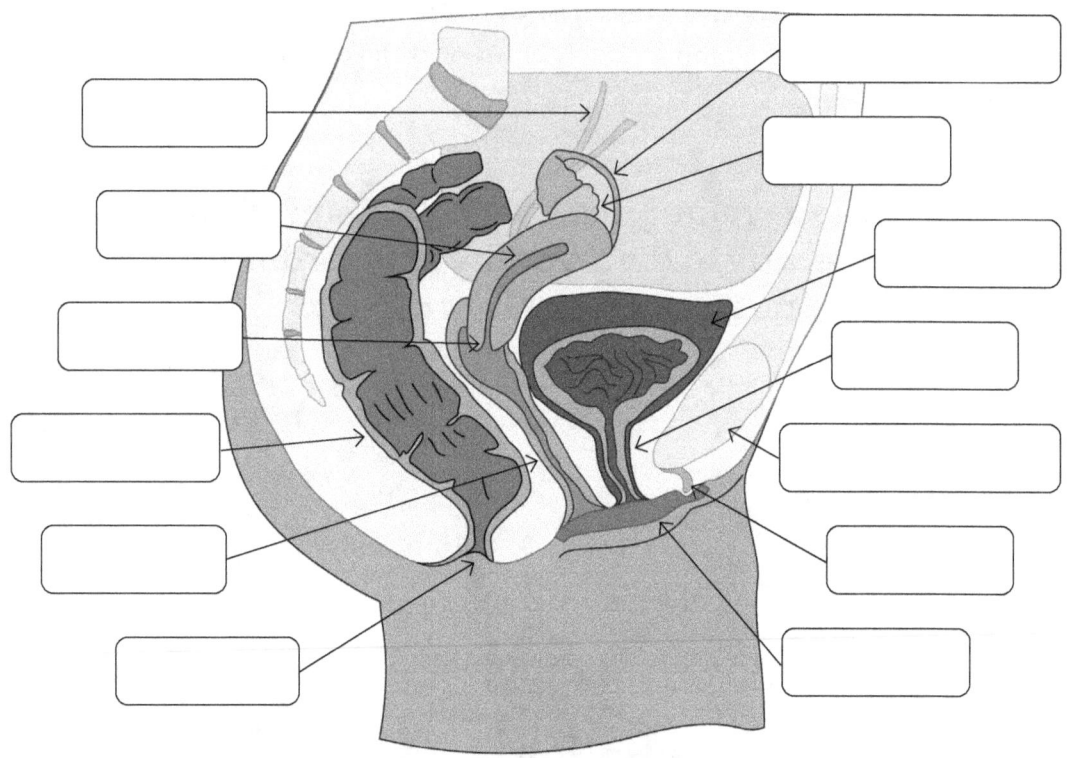

WORD BANK

Ureter   Bladder   Anus
Labium   Rectum   Uterus
Cervix   Clitoris   Pubic bone
Fallopian tube Vagina
Ovary   Urethra

THE FEMALE BODY - BOTTOM VIEW

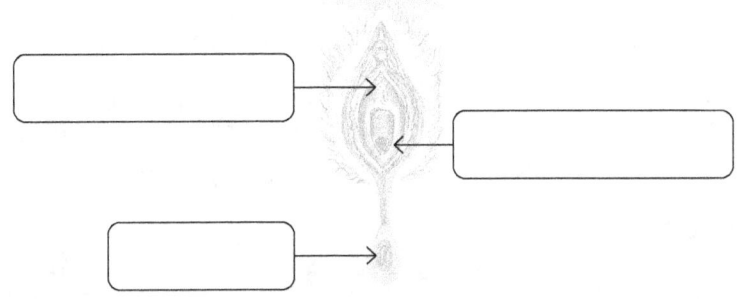

WORD BANK

Anus   Vagina   Urethra

THE FEMALE REPRODUCTIVE SYSTEM - FRONT VIEW

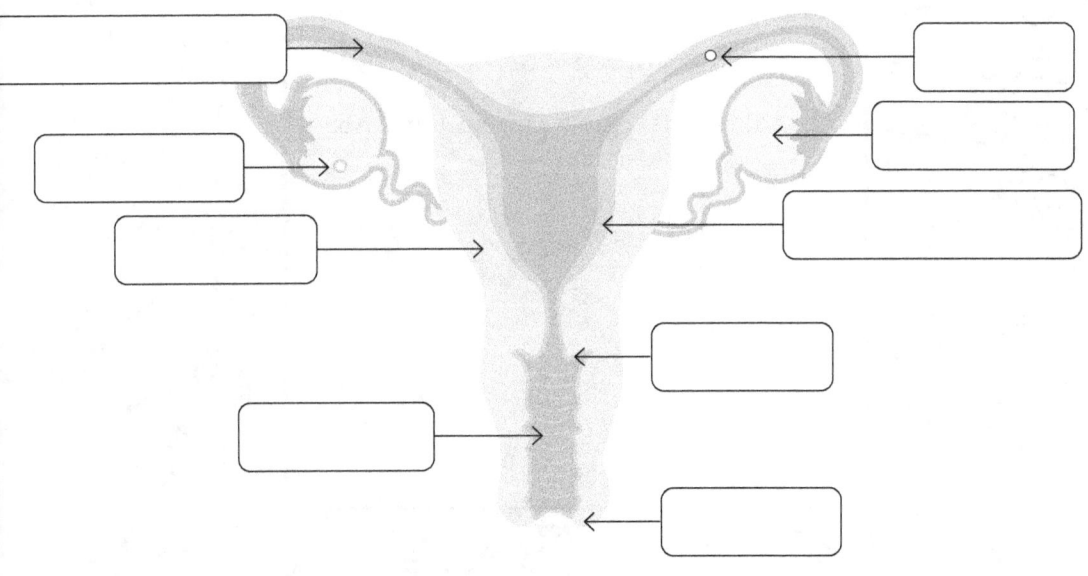

WORD BANK

Ovaries   Fallopian tube   Cervix
Ovum   Uterus   Vagina
Follicles   Endometrium   Vulva

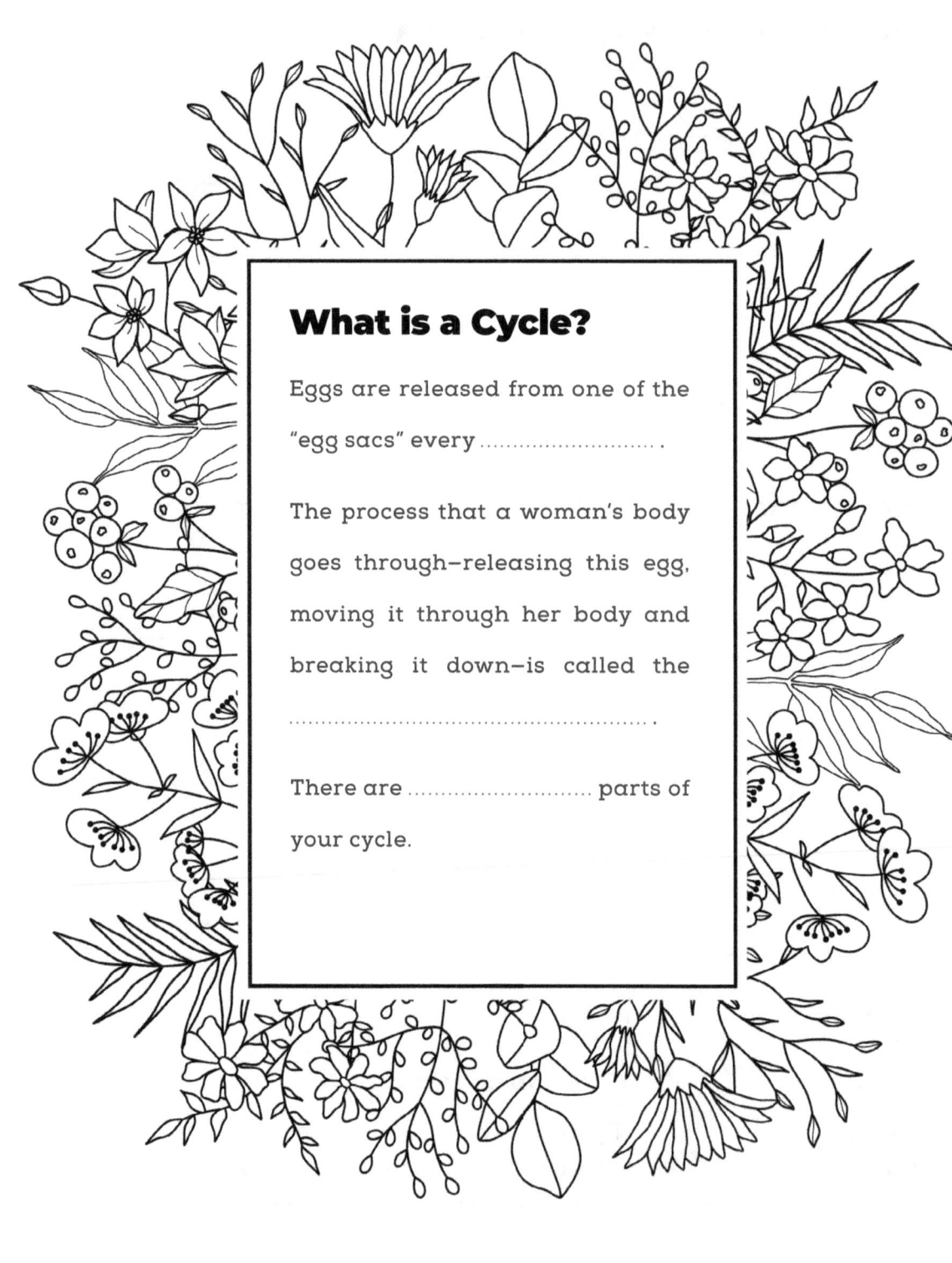

What is a Cycle?

Eggs are released from one of the "egg sacs" every ....

The process that a woman's body goes through—releasing this egg, moving it through her body and breaking it down—is called the ....

There are .... parts of your cycle.

Spring FOLLICULAR PHASE

How long does it last?

.... days

What happens during this stage?

___ ___ ___ ___ ___ ___ ___ . During this stage, one .... is preparing

to release an ....

What happens here is mostly (circle one)

invisible   **visible**

What is happening in the uterus?

Inside   you,   the   lining   of   the   uterus   ....   and

....

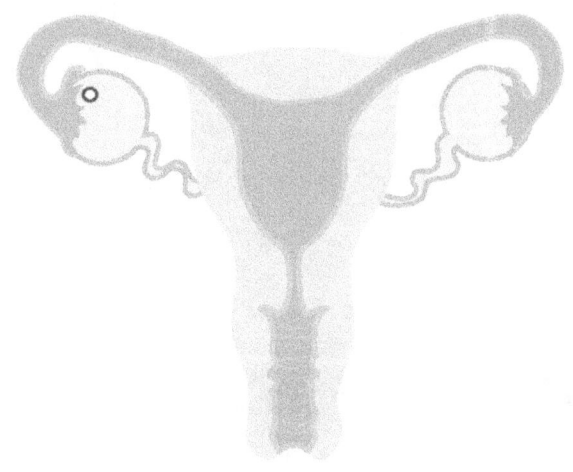

Summer **OVULATION**

How long does it last?

.... days

What happens during this stage?

___ ___ ___ ___ ___ ___ ___ ___ . In this stage, the .... actually is released

from its sac and travels through the .... to the

....

You will be able to detect the presence of ....

when it begins.

What happens here is mostly (circle one)

invisible   **visible**

What is happening in the uterus?

The lining of the .... continues to ....

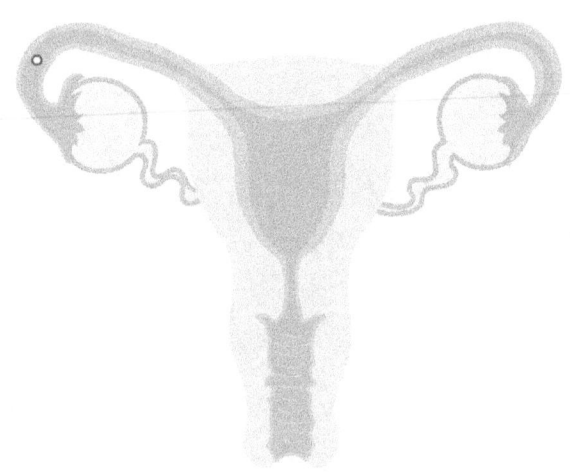

Autumn
LUTEAL PHASE

How long is this stage?

.... days

What happens during this stage?

___ ___ ___ ___ ___ ___ ___. The .... within the uterus begins to disintegrate

and the .... of the .... prepares to be shed.

Most women have little to no .... At the end of the stage,

some women experience...................... as the body prepares for menstruation.

What happens here is mostly (circle one)

invisible   **visible**

What is happening in the uterus?

As ovulation ends the discharge changes from clear to. .... At the

end of this phase the .... begins to fall off in pieces.

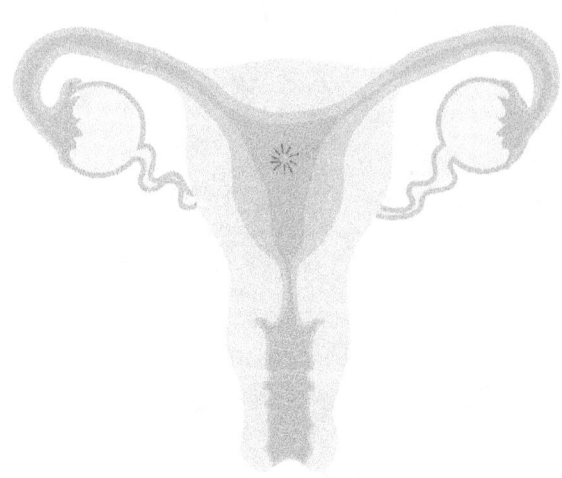

Winter
MENSTRUATION

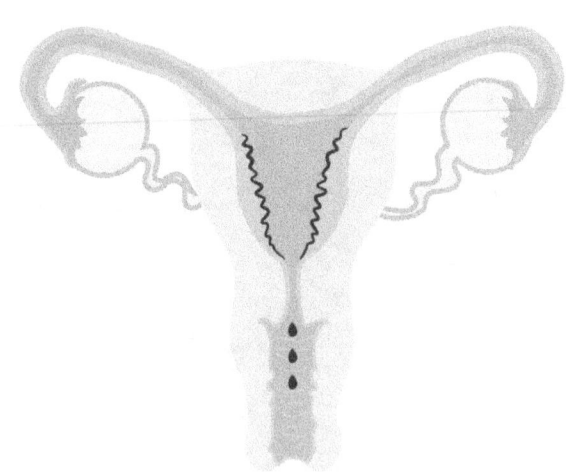

How long does it last?

.... days

What happens during this stage?

__ __ __ __ __ __ __ __ __ . The .... is washed out of your body. This is the most .... part of your cycle. It is the .... of the entire process.

What happens here is mostly (circle one)

                invisible   **visible**

What is happening in the uterus?

The .... breaks off and flows through your .... The blood that is shed is about .... to .... tablespoons overall.

Renewing our Minds

How does the world see a woman's cycle?

- ....
- ....
- ....

Women need to .... to their bodies.

What is the actual role of blood in the Bible?

Blood .... ! It is life giving!

Being a Catholic Christian means that we .... in Our

.... design for our

bodies.

So God created mankind in His own image,
in the image of God He created them;
male and female He created them.

....God saw all that He had made, and it was very good.

GENESIS 1:27

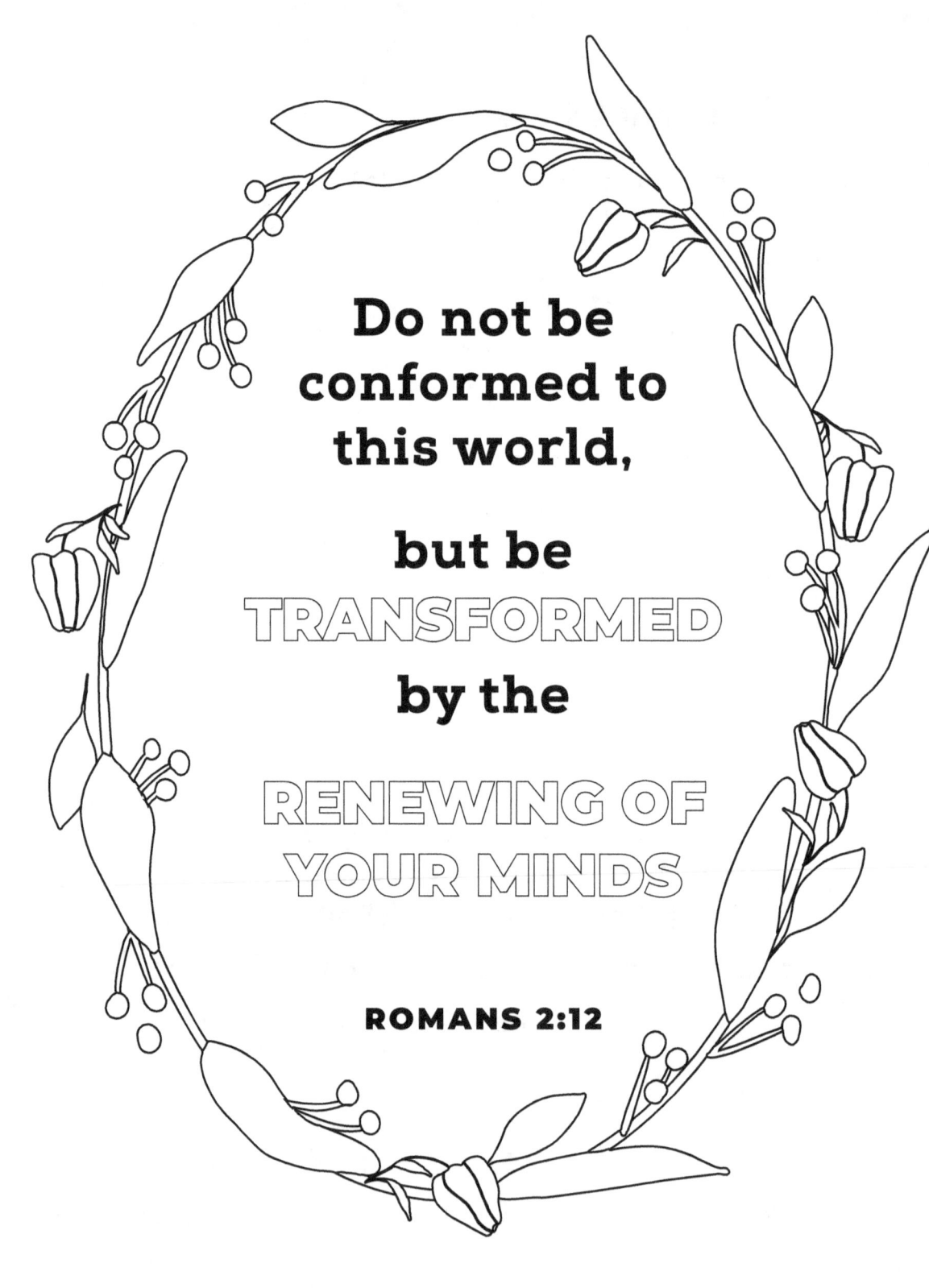

Do not be conformed to this world,

but be

TRANSFORMED

by the

RENEWING OF YOUR MINDS

ROMANS 2:12

Getting Gear for our Cycle

Gear: anything that helps collect menstrual flow either inside of our bodies or outside. Try to choose gear that is natural, chemical-free, and (if possible) reusable.

OUTSIDE

Disposable Pads

Pros	Cons
....	....
....	....
....	

Cloth pads

Pros	Cons
....	....
....	....
....	....

Period Panties

Pros	Cons
....	....
....	....
....	....

Tampons

Pros	Cons
....	....
....	....
....	....

Keeper Cups

Pros	Cons
....	....
....	....
....	....

Sponges

Pros	Cons
....	....
....	....
....	....

Interview Your Mom

Now's your chance to talk with your mom or mentor about her experience of menstruation. You can ask her any question you like, but here are a few suggestions.

When did you start your cycle? How old were you?

....

....

....

What was it like for you? How did you feel?

....

....

....

Do you still have your cycle? If not, when did you stop having it?

....

....

....

Have you ever had any problems with your cycle?

....

....

....

These questions can be important for you in the future because chances are that your cycle might be like your mom's.

For it was You who formed my inward parts;
You knit me together in my mother's womb.

I praise You, for I am fearfully and
wonderfully made.
Wonderful are Your works; that I know very well.

My frame was not hidden from You,
when I was being made in secret,
intricately woven in the depths of the earth.

PSALM 139:13-15

The Care and Feeding of Emotions

In our last session, we learned about how a woman's cycle is designed by God to work. Now we're going to add in another layer: our hormones and emotions!

"Therefore, behold, I will allure her,
and bring her into the wilderness,
and speak tenderly to her."

HOSEA 2:1

What are hormones?

Hormones are the .... in your

body that communicate and coordinate processes to your organs and

tissues.

Some of the body processes that hormones regulate:

- ....
- ....
- ....
- ....
- ....
- ....

INTRODUCING *Este,*

REPRESENTING ESTROGEN!

What does she do?

....

....

....

....

AND NOW... *Proge,*

STANDING IN FOR PROGESTERONE!

Here are her talents...

....

....

....

....

The Body/Feeling Connection

When you recognize that the seasons of your cycle can affect your mood, this can give you freedom!

Let's review the stages and talk about how you may feel during them.

FOLLICULAR PHASE

How might you feel during this stage?

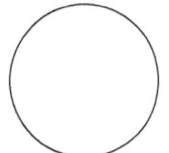 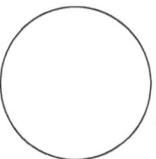 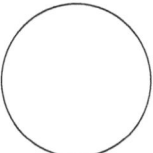 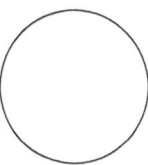

How can you take care of yourself during this stage?

You have lots of positive energy at this time. How can you use this energy to learn and grow during this time?

- ....
- ....
- ....
- ....

 **OVULATION**

How might you feel during this stage?

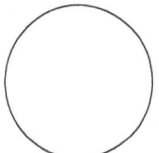 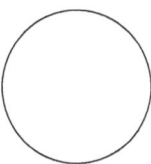 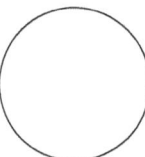 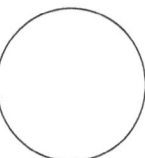

How can you take care of yourself during this stage?

Use your extra energy by focusing on something that's challenging. What are some things that you like to do that use energy?

- ....
- ....
- ....
- ....

LUTEAL PHASE

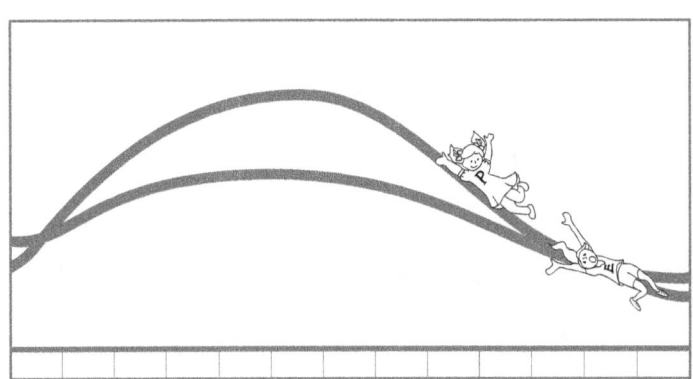

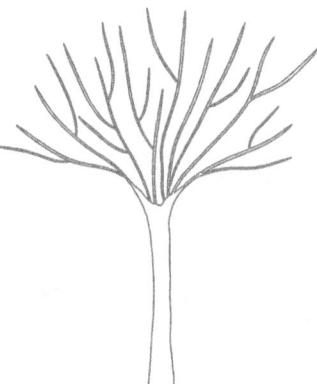

How might you feel during this stage?

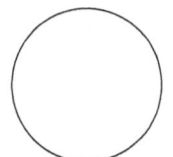 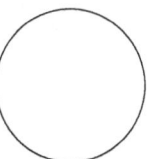 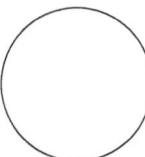 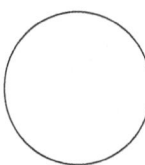

How can you take care of yourself during this stage?

For most of this time, you will feel "normal" and mellow, but at the end you may experience PMS. What can you do to support your body?

- ....
- ....
- ....
- ....

How might you feel during this stage?

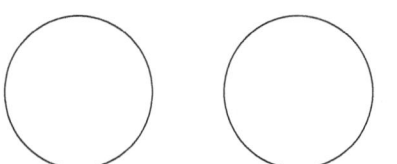 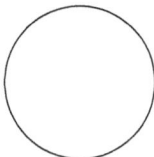 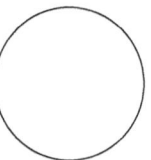

How can you take care of yourself during this stage?

During this stage, you will have the least amount of energy and drive. How can you nurture your body?

- ....
- ....
- ....
- ....

Tracking Your Cycle

Fill in the chart below to track how estrogen and progesterone behave during your cycle. Color the lines and mark them with an E or P.

Follicular Phase	Ovulation	Luteal Phase	Menstruation

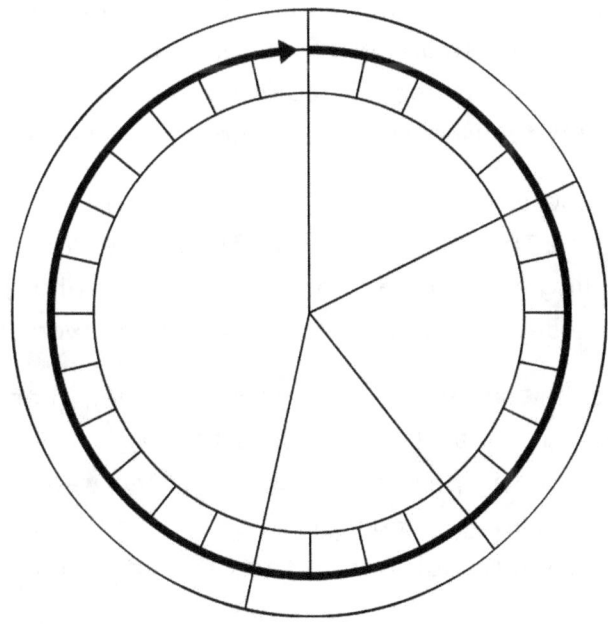

ORDER OF TRACKING YOUR CYCLE USING "OFFICIAL COUNTING"

Menstruation   Follicular Phase   Ovulation   Luteal Phase

My Personal Proverbs Chart

One tool we have found useful is the Personal Proverbs Chart created by Doran Richards. It is a way to both track your cycle and focus on a specific prayer intention for each stage. The chart uses the book of Proverbs from the Bible and four different colored markers. It's coded, so it's discreet if your chart is kept in a more public place.

1. For the season of **Menstruation**, we'll use the RED marker, since red reminds us of blood and Christ's saving death. When Day 1 of your flow arrives, use a red marker to write in "1" on that weekday and then read the first chapter of Proverbs. If any verse jumps out at you, read it again and think about what it means for your life. Write the number of the verse on that day of the chart. On Day 2, read the 2nd chapter of Proverbs, the 3rd chapter on Day 3, and so on until your period is over. Each day, you could also mark if your flow is heavy, medium or light. Reading your Proverbs will help you stay focused during this more difficult part of your cycle.

2. After your period is over, change the color to GREEN which stands for growing new life. This is the **Follicular Stage** or spring stage when your uterus is building a new lining and estrogen is climbing. Continue with numbering the days and recording the significant verses for yourself.

3. When you begin **Ovulation** (the Summer stage), change the color to PINK to represent joy and gladness. As the egg travels to your uterus, your estrogen will be peaking, so you may feel rather good. You will know you are ovulating when you notice mucus that is slippery, wet, or elastic. Continue with numbering the days and recording verses that speak to you.

4. When Ovulation is over, you will enter the **Luteal Phase** so you can start to write your numbers in ORANGE or YELLOW to stand for richness, abundance, and the fire of the Holy Spirit. This is the longest phase and at the end, you may experience some premenstrual signs which could be uncomfortable. Estrogen is decreasing so this may cause mood swings

or feeling down. Use your chart and the Proverbs to develop extra focus as you work to cast on your burdens on the One Who cares for you.

Note: You may not get through all 31 chapters of the book of Proverbs every month and that's ok! The beauty of this exercise is that you will have the opportunity to read the Scriptures from a different perspective every time. You may choose to not start with Proverbs 1 on Day 1 every month so you can occasionally get through to the end of the book. Just keep track by writing the chapter you are reading on your chart.

Enter more fully into hearing God's word and plan through using this tool!

"It can thus be said that women, by looking to Mary, find in her the secret of living their femininity with dignity and of achieving their own true advancement."

REDEMPTORIS MATER, 5

Managing Your Emotions

Emotions are terrible.. But they are fantastic

....

A woman's connection to her emotions is a great..........................to the world.

> "Thank you, every woman, for the simple fact of being a woman! Through the insight which is so much a part of your womanhood you enrich the world's understanding and help to make human relations more honest and authentic."
>
> **JOHN PAUL II, *LETTER TO WOMEN***

Anxiety

Steps to experiencing anxiety:

- Our brains perceive a ....

- Our body ....

- Responses may include .... , ... ,

  or .... , ...

- We can change our ....

- This will change our body's ....

Exercises for Mental Health

HAPPY PLACE

- Close your eyes and take a few deep breaths.

- **Think of the feeling you want to have.** Do you want to be happy? Excited? Calm? Energized?

- **Now imagine a place where you would feel that way.** Think of a setting that evokes the feelings that you would like to have. It could be a real place like a forest or a beach or it could be an imaginary place.

- What are the things that you see? What are the sounds that you hear? What do you feel like?

- **Now take a "snapshot" of this memory.** When we do this, we can go back to that picture to evoke these feelings whenever you would like to.

THREE THINGS

This is a great exercise when you are worrying about things in the future or something that happened in the past. We need to take time to focus on the present. That is where we are and where God is!

- **Notice three things that you see.** Look around you and see the details and colors in the items that are around you.

- **Notice three things that you hear.** If it's quiet maybe you hear the wind, or distant cars, or birds.

- **Notice three things that you physically feel.** Maybe it's your clothing, where you are sitting, or the air on your face.

- Repeat as needed to regain focus and peace.

Social Media: Warning!

Social media hurts your .... and .... development.

Connect with friends using .... , ... , and

....

When to Get Help

Get help if sadness is preventing you from ....

.... Talk to .... about how you

feel.

If you or a friend ever have thoughts of hurting yourself, you should

....

The national suicide prevention number to call or text for help is 988.

The Importance of Prayer

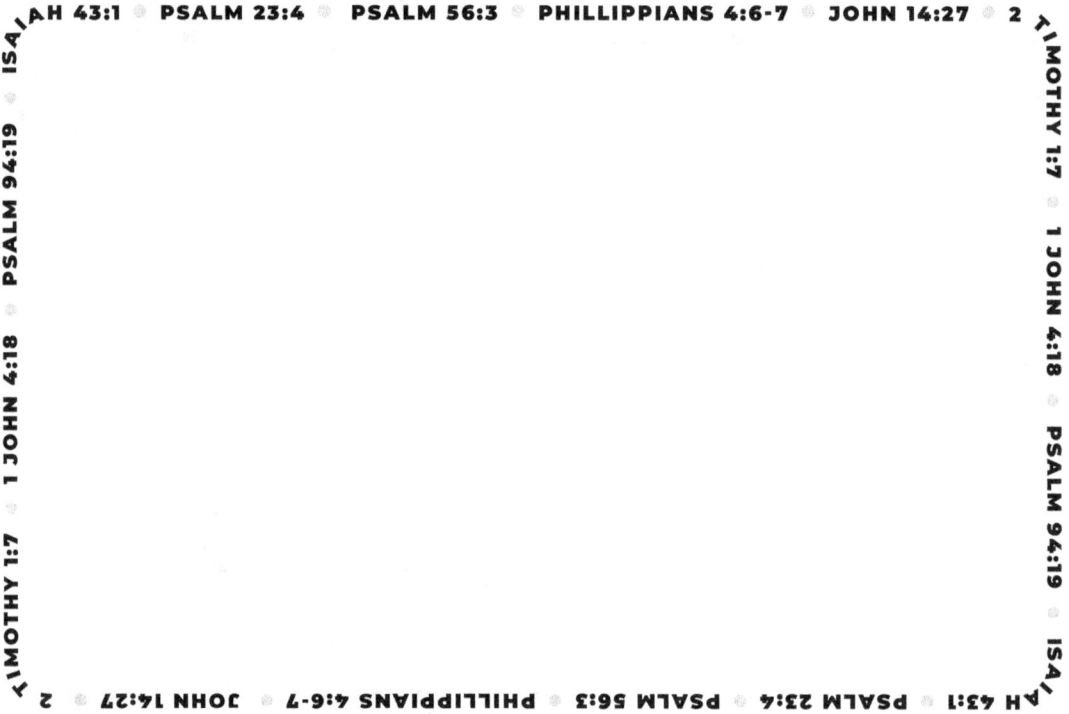

ISAIAH 43:1 • PSALM 23:4 • PSALM 56:3 • PHILLIPPIANS 4:6-7 • JOHN 14:27 • 2 TIMOTHY 1:7 • 1 JOHN 4:18 • PSALM 94:19 • ISAIAH 43:1 • PSALM 23:4 • JOHN 14:27 • PHILLIPPIANS 4:6-7 • PSALM 56:3 • PSALM 94:19 • 1 JOHN 4:18 • TIMOTHY 1:7 • 2

"The difficulties of life do not have to be unbearable. It is the way we look at them—through faith or unbelief— that makes them seem so. We must be convinced that our Father is full of love for us and that He only permits trials to come our way for our own good."

BROTHER LAWRENCE,
THE PRACTICE OF THE PRESENCE OF GOD

Interview Your Mom

Do/did your moods change during your cycle?

....
....
....
....

How did you take care of yourself during your cycle?

....
....
....
....

What place does prayer have in your life?

....
....
....
....

Do you have a favorite scripture?

....
....
....
....

O Lord, You have searched me and known me.
You know when I sit down and when I rise up;
You discern my thoughts from far away.

You search out my path and my lying down,
and are acquainted with all my ways.

Even before a word is on my tongue,
O Lord, You know it completely....

...Search me, O God, and know my heart;
test me and know my thoughts.

PSALM 139:1-4, 23

Let's Talk About Change

When we begin our cycle, it's not just our hormones that change: it's many other things as well! God prepares us for the great work of bringing new life into the world. This means that we grow taller and stronger: our breasts which are used to nurse babies will grow larger. The parts of our bodies that are involved in birth grow protective hair. This means we need to take extra care of our bodies and treat them with the respect they deserve.

"When the body is seen as mere matter, anything goes. The body, however, isn't mere matter. That's modernist fiction. Rather, as the Catholic anthropology of the Theology of the Body reminds us, man is a union of body and soul, made in the image of God. Which means our bodies are us. Your body is you. My body is me."

EMILY STIMPSON,
THESE BEAUTIFUL BONES, PG 27

Breast Development

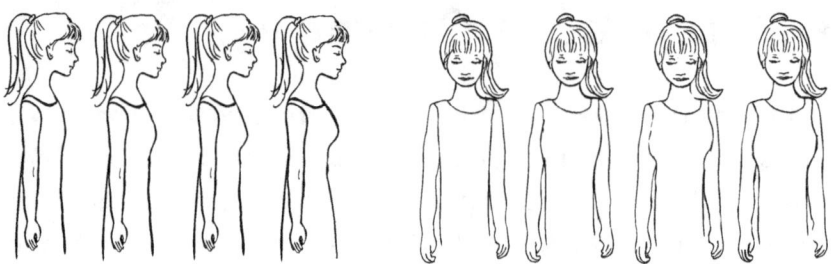

THE CHANGE: ....

YOUR RESPONSE: ....

Bras can help with your ....

Bras .... your ....

Bras protect your ....

Bras help you look more ....

Every woman should have .... bras

Bras last ....

More hair, everywhere! (not really)

THE CHANGE: ....

YOUR RESPONSE: ....

Places that hair will begin to grow longer and coarser:

- ● ....
- ● ....
- ● ....

Sweet Scents

THE CHANGE: ....

YOUR RESPONSE: ....

Three things you can do to smell good:

- ....
- ....
- ....

Skin Changes (the least fun part of growing up)

THE CHANGE: ....

YOUR RESPONSE:

- ....
- ....
- ....

Sleeping Like a Baby

THE CHANGE: ....

Effects of lack of sleep:

- ....
- ....
- ....
- ....

THE SOLUTION: ....

Teenagers should get .... hours of sleep a night!

Ways you can help yourself go to sleep

- ● ....
- ● ....
- ● ....
- ● ....

Growing: A Good Excuse to Go Shopping!

THE CHANGE: Growth in ...., ..., ...

YOUR RESPONSE: ...., ...

Take a minute to practice standing with a good posture. Stand with your feet parallel and directly below your hips. Take time to feel your feet and balance your weight evenly across them. Your shoulders, hips and ankles should all be in a straight line. Lengthen your neck and think of making space between your head and your pelvis. Make sure you stand with your shoulders down and back. Simply standing tall can lift our mood and make us feel more confident!

Body Image and the Lilies of the Field

All flowers are .... but have a .... beauty! All

bodies are .... but have a .... beauty!

Ways you are unique

- ....

- ....

- ....

- ....

- ....

When we .... ourselves to other women this can lead to

.... or ....

Make sure you .... for your body in a way that

.... your unique design!

Which Flower are You?

God didn't just make one kind of flower: He literally made thousands! In this, Our Father God shows us that **there is not just one way to be beautiful**: there are immense possibilities!

Think about yourself as a flower. If you were a flower, what kind would you be?

How are you similar to your mom? Your sisters? How are you different?

If you like, pick or draw yourself a flower that represents the kind of beauty you have, or want to have. Let your imagination go and have fun!

Here are some ideas:

- How many petals would you have? Would you have lots of blossoms on one stem, like a hydrangea, or just have one showstopping floret, like a sunflower?

- Where do you grow? In the wild, in a garden with your family and friends, in a house?

- How many seeds would you have? What color would your leaves be?

Create or share a picture of your flower. Give three reasons why you picked this flower and how it's like you.

For inspiration, here are just a few of the huge varieties of flowers that God has created, often together with people. Many of these flowers are used to honor Our Lady as well!

Share your picture with your mom, and thank God for His beautiful creations, including the beauty He is creating in and through you!

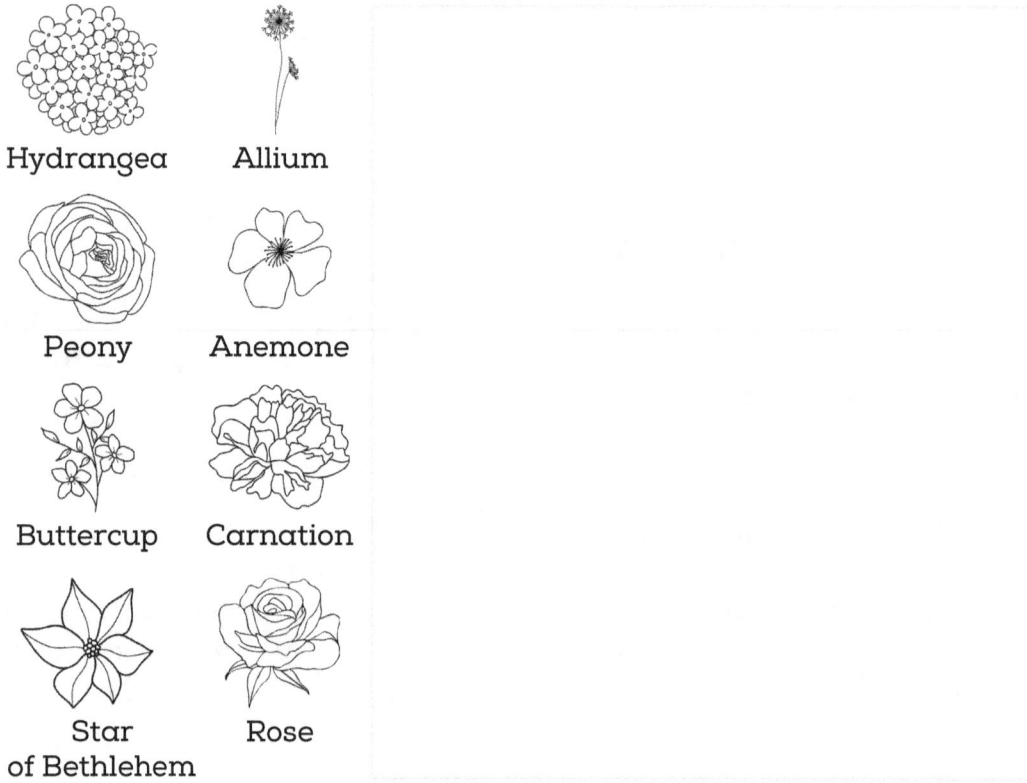

Hydrangea   Allium

Peony   Anemone

Buttercup   Carnation

Star of Bethlehem   Rose

Interview Your Mom

Your mom was a girl just like you!
Put a picture of her here:

Now, ask your mom some questions to learn more about her!
Mom, when you were my age....

- Who was your best friend? ....

- What was your favorite ice cream? ....

- What were you really good at? ....

- What was your favorite color? ....

- What did you do with your friends? ....

- What was your favorite thing to wear? ....

What of these things has changed? What has stayed the same?

....

....

....

....

....

"Where can I go from Your spirit?
Or where can I flee from Your presence?

If I ascend to heaven, You are there;
if I make my bed in Sheol, You are there.

If I say, "Surely the darkness shall cover me,
and the light around me become night,"

even the darkness is not dark to You;
the night is as bright as the day,
for darkness is as light to You."

PSALM 139: 7-8, 11-12

Caring for our Body, a Temple of the Holy Spirit

Let's take a deep dive into how to take care of yourself through diet, exercise, and hydration. Remember that because you are young, it's easier for you to start making healthy changes for yourself. The choices you make today can form habits for a lifetime!

Nutrition

Three macronutrients

- ....
- ....
- ....

Draw a healthy plate here:

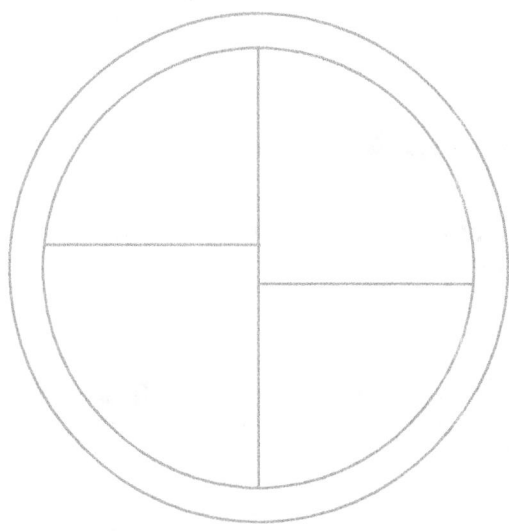

PORTION SIZE: EVERYTHING IN MODERATION

Your stomach is the same size as your ....

Get a "Hand"-le on Portion Control

Palm: 3-4 oz of meat, salty snacks or whole grains

Tip of finger: teaspoon of salt, oil or butter

Fist: 1 cup of veggies

Thumb: 2 tablespoons of healthy fats

You should choose foods that are .... over foods with ....

How to Make Healthy Choices: Supporting Your Cycle

There's a chart at the end of the chapter to fill out. The first three rows are review: see what you remember from previous chapters! Yes, it's ok to peek.

Rethink Your Drink

Milk is important because it gives you .... and ....

The best thing you can drink is ....!

Benefits of water:

- ....

- ....

- ....

Four herbs (among many!) that can help you during menstruation are

- ....
- ....
- ....
- ....

Exercise

Fill out the chart on p. 54 with some suggestions on what to do during the different seasons of your cycle.

When Things Go Wrong

Amenorrhea

- Amenorrhea is ....
  ....
  ....

- Girls should get their period by the age of ....

- When you start your period, it shouldn't stop for more than .... months

- It's important for women to have proper amount of ....
  ....in our diet and to maintain a healthy ....

- Three things you can do if you experience amenorrhea

  ○ ....

  ○ ....

  ○ ....

Dysmenorrhea

- Dysmenorrhea is ....

....

....

- Should you miss school/work/activities because you have your period? ....

- What are some symptoms of dysmenorrhea in addition to pain?

  ○ ....

  ○ ....

  ○ ....

  ○ ....

  ○ ....

- What are some supplements/medications you can take that may help?

  ○ ....

  ○ ....

  ○ ....

  ○ ....

  ○ ....

Menorrhagia

- Menorrhagia is ....

....

....

- Normally, your period should not last more than .... days

- Tell your mom if you soak more than .... pad or tampon in .... hour.

Irregular Bleeding

- It is not normal to have periods that are less than .... days apart or more than .... days on a regular basis.

- A common cause of irregular bleeding is ____ ____ ____ ____ or ....

- This is why is it important to track your ....

Endometriosis

- Endometriosis is ....

- Symptoms of endometriosis

  ○ ....

  ○ ....

  ○ ....

  ○ ....

- Three things that may help

  ○ Take ....

  ○ Eat ....

  ○ Eliminate .... and ....

General Health

Always find a doctor who .... !

If you are unsure of a treatment get a ....

	FOLLICULAR PHASE	OVULATION	LUTEAL PHASE	MENSTRUATION
ESTE + PROGE				
DAYS				
FEELINGS	○ ○	○	○ ○ ○ ○	○ ○
EAT				
DO				

Interview Your Mom

What was your worst cooking disaster?

....
....
....

What is a food that you hated when you were my age that you
actually like now?

....
....
....

Since you started your cycle, are there any problems that you
had? How did you deal with them?

....
....
....
....

Make a list of new foods or recipes that you would like to try!

....
....
....
....

My bones are not hidden from You,
when I was being made in secret,
fashioned in the depths of the earth.

Your eyes saw me unformed;
in Your book all are written down;
my days were shaped, before one came to be.

How precious to me are Your designs,
O God; how vast the sum of them!

Were I to count them,
they would outnumber the sands;
when I complete them, still You are with me

PSALM 139:13-15

Celebrating Womanhood!

Our clothes reveal what we think about ourselves—as people and as a culture. That's why styles change, because ideas change! As Catholics, we need to make sure that we are not being shaped by the secular ideas around us, but that we are continually "transformed by the renewal of our minds" and that includes our clothing choices.

"In the light of Mary, the Church sees in the face of women the reflection of a beauty which mirrors the loftiest sentiments of which the human heart is capable:

the self-offering totality of love;

the strength that is capable of bearing the greatest sorrows;

limitless fidelity and tireless devotion to work;

the ability to combine penetrating intuition with words of support and encouragement."

JOHN PAUL II, *REDEMPTORIS MATER*

Beauty and Fashion

> "The body, in fact, and only the body,
> is capable of making visible what is
> invisible: the spiritual and the divine."
>
> **ST. JOHN PAUL, FEBRUARY 20 1980**

Our clothes reveal what we think about ....

The best person to talk to about modesty is ....

HOW YOU DRESS MANIFESTS YOUR SOUL

Clothing should show that you love being a ....

We should not use clothing to .... ourselves.

What we wear should be an expression of what we ....

about ....

HOW YOU DRESS COMMUNICATES TO OTHERS ABOUT YOU

Style is a tool for ....

HOW YOU DRESS IS A FORM OF POSITIVE "SELF-TALK"

We can communicate to .... through our dress.

The Five Style Personalities

(https://stylecoachinginstitute.com/mini-personal-styling-masterclass-style-personalities/)

Here are five different ways of expressing yourself through clothes. We feel most confident when our clothing reflects who we are and not who we wish we could be or admire in others. Check out these five "style personalities" and see of one of them resonates with you!

CREATIVE

- Fun, creative pieces that mix and match
- Jewelry is bold and modern
- Eye-catching statement accessories
- Strong bright colors
- Different than everyone else
- People never know what you will wear
- Unusual lines and shapes
- Lots of different types of clothes
- Makeup is experimental and new
- Finds styles at thrift stores, bohemian, modern, boutiques

DRAMATIC

- Striking colors and large prints
- Priority is the "wow" factor
- Clothing is not necessarily practical, but stylish
- Dramatic makeup
- Tend to be overdressed than underdressed
- Don't mind attracting the attention of others
- Metallic, animal prints or shiny material
- Bold, well-styled and confident
- Finds styles at Forever 21, Urban Outfitters, Anthropologie

NATURAL

- Comfort is key
- Easy to wear and not "fussy"
- Simple lines and basic colors
- Jewelry includes wood, shell, stones, natural materials
- Don't like being over-dressed
- Minimal to no makeup
- Accessories are few and understated
- Anything eye-catching is just a detail, not a main piece
- Tend to neutrals and natural fabrics like brown leather, linen, and cotton
- Finds styles at Old Navy, Lands End, American Eagle, Express, Aeropostale

ROMANTIC

- Feminine, pretty colors like pastels
- Details include ruffles, lace, and appliques
- Material tends to be full and drapey
- Soft lines with bust or waist definition
- Patterns are subtle, floral, and understated
- Like to wear perfume and subtle makeup
- Prefer skirts and dresses to pants
- Finds styles at Petal Lush, Vera Wang, Baltic Born, April Cornell

CLASSIC

- Timeless look
- Quality over quantity
- Smart, understated, designed to not attract attention
- Soft folds and straight lines
- Tailored and not baggy or loose
- Prefer pants to jeans or sweats
- Colors all match in classic combinations
- Classic shoe styles
- Makeup is safe and predictable
- Find styles at Ann Taylor, Nordstrom, White House Black Market

What do I like to wear? What is my Style Personality?

....

....

....

RESOURCES FOR YOU!

Check out some of these Catholic women and what they are doing to provide tools and ideas for communicating truth by how we dress!

- LillianFallon.com

- NicoleMCaruso.com

- LitanyNYC.com

- MeghanAshleyStyling.com

- TelosArtShop.com

- Siena-Co.com Swimwear

- Catholic Dress Co.

> "Do not adorn yourselves outwardly by braiding your hair, and by wearing gold ornaments or fine clothing; rather, let your adornment be the inner self with the lasting beauty of a gentle and quiet spirit, which is very precious in God's sight."
>
> **1 PETER 3:3-4**

Progress usually tends to be measured according to the criteria of science and technology...

Much more important is the social and ethical dimension, which deals with human relations and spiritual values.

In this area...society certainly owes much to the

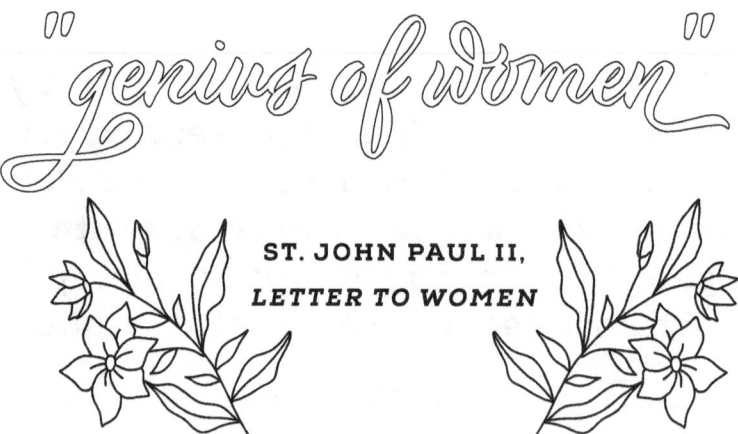

"*genius of women*"

ST. JOHN PAUL II,
LETTER TO WOMEN

You Are Not Alone

Community of Women

.... made men and women equal in the Church.

Women are equal in .... to men, and their .... are necessary in the world.

Don't be fooled by those who say that in order to have worth you need to act like a ....

The Importance of Friendships

Friendships are a gift from God, but they need to be .... , ... and ....

One thing that destroys friendship is ....

The three gates of speech are

- Is it .... ?
- Is it .... ?
- Is it .... ?

When we put Christ first we can build genuine ....

> "May the words of my mouth and the meditation of my heart be pleasing in your sight, O Lord, my Rock and my Redeemer."
>
> **PSALM 19:14**

Your family

You are here because of the .... who came before you.

List the women in your life who are important to you:

- ....
- ....
- ....
- ....

MY FAMILY HISTORY.....

Choose one of the women above to interview. Put a star next to the oldest woman. I bet she can tell you some interesting facts that you didn't know! If you can, do a family tree as well and find out about the women who came three or four generations before you.

Fill out the next four pages by interviewing two living relatives and learning about two relatives who have already died.

Women in my life

Name: ....

How we are related: ....

Date of birth: ....

Place of birth: ....

Age of marriage: ....

Years married: ....   Number of children: ....

Profession or talents: ....

Favorite thing to do when they were my age: ....

Best thing about being a woman ....

Advice: ....

....

My questions for her: ....

....

....

....

Women in my life

Name: ....

How we are related: ....

Date of birth: ....

Place of birth: ....

Age of marriage: ....

Years married: .... Number of children: ....

Profession or talents: ....

Favorite thing to do when they were my age: ....

Best thing about being a woman ....

Advice: ....

....

My questions for her: ....

....

....

....

Women who came before me

Name: ....

How we are related: ....

Date of birth: ....

Place of birth: ....

Age of marriage: ....

Years married: .... Number of children: ....

Year of death: ....

Profession or talents: ....

Interesting facts: ....

....

What do I wish I could ask her? ....

....

....

....

....

Women who came before me

Name: ....

How we are related: ....

Date of birth: ....

Place of birth: ....

Age of marriage: ....

Years married: ....   Number of children: ....

Year of death: ....

Profession or talents: ....

Interesting facts: ....

....

What do I wish I could ask her? ....

....

....

....

....